Bharat S. Shah, M.D. presents

I0473800

CAPITALISM
THE COLONIZATION OF AMERICA

And the Mating Behavior of
the Praying Mantis

Setubandh Publications
New York

Capitalism,
The colonization of America, and
The mating behavior of the praying mantis

ISBN# 13: 978-1467909105
          10:     1467909106

First edition 2012

U. S. $ 8.00

Please see the end pages for
other books by the author

❖

Dedicated to
all the unemployed,
those deprived of their benefits,
the later day homeless, the uninsured,
the almost retirees,
and others who got broke
after sacrificing everything they had,
on the altar of
the merciless almighty Capitalism!

And to my late father
Who taught me not to surrender
our common sense to the expert opinion

❖

PREFACE

The Declaration of Independence tells us that people tend to bear things as long as they are bearable. However, the catastrophic financial debacle that we have been suffering through has proved that we also continue to bear things that are unbearable. It is one thing to depose a foreign tyrant, but it is quite another to find out the one amongst us, especially if that is in any way connected to traditions held sacred for ages.

There comes a time when we have to acknowledge that people and institutions are not what we had thought them to be, but are doing exactly the opposite of what they were meant to do. It is painful to come to grips with the reality that it is our own guard who is burglarizing our house.

Declaring independence from authorities worshiped by us thus far is a torment, physical, and emotional. However, riding a beast whose rein is not in our hands is a dangerous and unconscionable apathy.

Rising unemployment, homelessness, and the credit crunch are not supposed to be parts of the everyday vocabulary of the richest country in the world. Inability to confront these decisively is not becoming to the sole superpower of the world.

The USA has become like the giant Guliver, with our friends, allies, partners, enemies, and other Lilliputians crawling all over us. Our political and financial institutions are as if determined to block any meaningful action to resolve the crises.

The enemy amongst us is more dangerous, because it can be perceived as a friend, and may even be revered. We should be more decisive in doing away with that child-molesting dear uncle. Endless mutual finger pointing should make us suspect that maybe the real culprit is not identified yet.

Political parties and financial institutions certainly deserve to get some blame, but not all of it. Our own greed and actions or lack thereof deserve some, too. How come, suddenly all of us have become so bad? Well, we have not, and it is not as sudden as we may like to believe either.

Is it not possible that our financial system itself is tying up everything into knots? Maybe, Capitalism itself, so marvelously suitable for exploitation of the colonies, in its antiquated form is no more adequate or appropriate for independent, democratic nations of Europe and America?

The message of this book is, we need to reform, and replace if needed, Capitalism and establish a modern system that is just, fair, and not based entirely upon greed and exploitation. I am sure it can be done by all of us working together in good faith. No violence should erupt, unless one side or another refuses to listen to any other language.

I am not an economist but I do know that subject from being at the other end of the knife like the 99 percent of Americans. I have seen my 403(B) pension plan slowly melt away just as I retired. Admittedly I am more fortunate, albeit barely so, than many who have lost everything including their faith, future and hope for a better tomorrow for themselves and for their children.

As a physician I know a thing or two about diagnosing the ailment afflicting my patients, and by extrapolation, maybe, a nation. In these pages I will make the case that Capitalism has turned upon us, and reduced America to a mere colony. The sooner we tame it or run away from it, the better off we all will be.

Yes, it was a lovely shade tree once, but it is dangerously leaning over our house now. Our course of action should be obvious. We have heard, "It is the economy, stupid!" Change that to, "It is the stupid economic system!"

Understandably, I have oversimplified a very complex issue, and naively come up with some possible solutions. Naive these may be, irrational they are not.

I would like to thank Mr. Subodh Shah, Arun Bhansali, Michael Buttenhauser, Prof. Madhusudan Kapadia, Mahendra Shah for their invaluable comments and suggestions, not all of which are accepted. No endorsement of this work by them is implied.

Lastly I thank my wife of 42 years, Usha, who never let me feel poor, no matter how bad the times were.

Bharat S. Shah, M.D.
New York
<bhrtshah@yahoo.com>
January 16, 2012.

TABLE OF CONTENTS

My dad was a lower middle class merchant of lose tea in Mumbai (Bombay then), and had one free lance laborer and another employee, a 75 year old senior man.

When the business ran into trouble, thanks to natural and political turmoil, my dad got ill and felt compelled to close it. He did not even have to give one month's notice. However, he called the senior man, explained the situation to him, which the latter also knew well, and asked him to look for another job.

He did not lay him off, but continued to run the money losing business. The employee asked my dad to go ahead and close the business, without worrying about him. My dad replied that it would not be easy for the latter to find a job at his advanced age. Maybe, after six months or so, he landed a job, when my dad closed the shop, and went looking for a job for himself! He could afford to be rich, because he had no money.

1. INTRODUCTION

These United States of ours have lot to be proud of. In a short history spanning a little more than two hundred years, from a British colony, this country has managed to become the sole superpower of the world. Although far from being perfect, it has strived for many worthy causes at home and abroad.

Its leadership, loyalty to its allies, and its willingness and eagerness to help those struck with calamities have been exemplary. The best is its tenacity to come out of from being down under, fighting with great determination and prowess.

The Cassandras of doom have been predicting its downfall for quite some time, albeit rescheduling its demise repeatedly. Position of leadership and the power center of the world are slipping away from it, and some have begun to fear for obvious reasons and with great concern.

America has welcomed millions to its shores over the centuries, the present writer being one of the recent arrivals merely half a century ago. Not many countries in the world can boast that. America bashing has become a favorite pastime. There are cynics who do not see anything right with the country, while super patriots fail to see anything wrong with it at all. The cup is still at least half full.

Its institutions, by their sheer number alone have amazed foreigners. Its democratic institutions have been constantly striving to make it "a more perfect union." Its wealth is enviable. Its vast expanse, abundant natural resources, and thin population density have been its greatest blessings.

America's values, work ethic, and concern for the humanity, and for nature have kept it going. The Yankee ingenuity and innovativeness have brought home innumerable Nobel prizes. Various branches of its government have kept one another in balance. Its fourth estate, the free press has always kept its leaders on their toes.

Its Capitalist financial system has served it well in producing and accumulating enormous wealth over the years, and has allowed it to become the money lender of the world. It has survived two world wars, and many other large and protracted military engagements all over the globe.

There is no discernible reason to predict its downfall. In the last few years America has become like a trapped elephant, apparently tied up with flimsy weeds, or like superman without his crystal.

Our country lost its top credit rating, our financial system came to a grinding and screeching halt, the tug of war in the House and the Senate remained a tie, several financial houses collapsed, and people's own houses went into foreclosure.

If all these had occurred because we had run out of money, we would have shed a few tears and would have gotten used to our fate. Tens of millions of Americans are without any health insurance, employers are reluctant to hire workers for the fear of their future healthcare expense.

Granted, we are all selfish and greedy, but it is not conceivable that all of us, or even the top one percent, or a fraction thereof have suddenly become mean, callous, and apathetic.

There is a complex and intricate system of political, financial, religious, and social factors affecting your and my bottom lines.

2. ANATOMY OF OUR FINANCIAL SYSTEM

This is my limited understanding of our financial system and its working. It is not an extensive description written for an economics examination. There are many forms of economic systems. We will ignore differences among the terms like financial, fiduciary, fiscal, etc.

Communism is the most dreaded system here. It treats everybody's work as having equal value. All wealth belongs to the government of the working class, which doles it out to its populace in proportion to the work put in.

There is no right to hold private property. Moreover, there is very little freedom, and oppression is rampant. There is no right to dissent. There is no motivation to work harder, because benefit does not reward the effort.

Socialism is a milder form of Communism, and it treats people with dignity. Important services like post, telephone, telegraph, railways, and major industries and utilities are under direct control of the government. Good of society takes priority over that of the individual. Private property can be held, but controls abound.

Capitalism is the system of economy in the United States, and in several European countries. Varying degrees of the other two systems are mixed with it. Capitalism is a highly individualistic system, based on personal motivation and reward. Greed is not a taboo, but it is rather a virtue.

Free markets without any government interference is its main characteristic. Price of goods is what the market will bear, without any regard to the cost of producing them. Almost all services and industries are under private control, often with nominal official oversight.

Increasing the demands and expanding markets for selling goods is carried out by means of marketing, advertising, and other promotions. Profit is the sole purpose.

Lowest possible costs of production combined with low cost transportation, low taxes on goods, sales, and on net profits, generates abundant cash flows for more production of more products, more advertising dollars, and cash rewards for top managers and other bosses.

Employees may share profits, get bonuses, and fringe benefits. Companies are owned by individuals, families, a few partners, or by public at large. Publicly owned companies issue millions of chunks of partnership, each being appropriately called, a "share" of that company.

A *stock* ideally contains many shares and even a fraction thereof. That word is interchangeable with *share* in practice. These are traded on open market, which is popularly known as stock market, also known as Wall Street after its location in New York City.

Market value of a company's stock is determined by its performance and estimated profit for the future, among many other factors. Company may distribute a part of its profits to shareholders as yearly *dividends (income stocks)*. Some companies do not distribute dividends but instead, let the value of its stock grow. These are known as *growth stocks*.

Stocks and shares are also called owners' stake or *equity* in the company. Often companies may want to borrow money for short term without recruiting more partners. Then they issue *bonds, notes*, and other *commercial paper*. As opposed to equity, this is called *debt*. Buyers receive interest on them.

Bank is the oldest institution. It takes your deposits, gives you some interest, while earning lot more than that by pooling the cash and investing it for higher returns. It can invest in stocks, bonds, real estate, or lend money to companies and to individuals. The latter includes mortgages on our houses, and car loans.

The most lucrative lending by banks is as the credit card debt that we run up by swiping that plastic. Banks can charge 25-30% interest in some cases. Then there are fees of all kinds, and the ubiquitous penalties for over using, not using the card, or using too much or too little of their services. Other than toll booths, banks are the only place where you stand in line to give them your money. They are more visible in the neighborhoods.

Insurance companies sell you safety and security while you are alive, and subsequently to your loved ones. They protect your house, cars, and yourself against law suits. Essentially, they only distribute the losses of one person or an entity and spread them among a larger number to reduce the pain. If stock markets and banks trade on our greed and gluttony, insurance business trades on our fears, exaggerating them as needed.

Insurance companies also invest their surplus cash the way the banks do. Social Security and pension plans are also kinds of assurances. All three are heavily invested in the stock market.

Individuals like you and I may get lucky enough to have extra cash on hand, at least for a while, and we may also put it in the stock market. Thus all of us work together to provide stocks their antigravity boost with our collective conscience, or rather with greed without any conscience.

It is obvious from the above that there is reason enough for us to savor this rosy picture where everybody is protected against everything for ever, and we can lie down on our backs, and watch everything just keep going up, up, and without any fear of it going away, per chance.

3. THE MIGHTY OAK
THAT IS CAPITALISM

Ten scores and a few more years ago, our forefathers embraced Capitalism. They were descendants of the British, and had arrived in the land of abundance. Producing, amassing, and enjoying the wealth was an understandable goal. It was too dazzling for them to see the red coats of the people who gave Capitalism to us.

When we hear the word *slave*, we cannot think of our founding fathers being ones. Yes, America was a British colony, slave to the whims of its colonizers. Britannia ruled over a major part of the world, and the sun had to look for a place to set. Industrial revolution was taking place. Production of goods was increasing. New sources of raw materials and new markets to sell processed merchandize were needed.

Finding cheaper raw materials, transporting them inexpensively to England, processing them using the machinery, with minimum manual labor and to export them back to other countries, had generated lot of wealth for England.

The thirteen colonies were also exploited. England's attempt to force the tea from India on to the shores of the future USA ended in the Boston Tea Party. That was the last time a *tea party* did anything in favor of the common American people.

Books on economics give us differences among capital, principle, wealth, and other terms. For us, the word *money* will suffice. There have been many forms and shapes of money over the ages. Roman soldiers were paid in buckets of salt, and we still have to be *worth our salt*, to get our *salaries*.

Women, slaves, and animals were also considered as property, and were reported as hundred heads of cattle, etc. The Greek word for head is *caput*, our wealth was counted in heads, and hence we have the *Capitalism*.

Today we use metal coins, paper currency notes, checks, and plastic credit cards. The important change is that modern money like coins has no inherent value. They are objects of virtual value. They are shares of governments or other agencies issuing them and standing behind them.

It is not possible to cover the subject of Capitalism in a couple of pages here, but we will review it just enough to understand it. Capitalism is based on individual's right to make money, own it, and make it grow. It does not believe in distributing wealth among the rich and the poor, unlike Communism, nor does it advance the greater good at the expense of an individual, unlike Socialism.

Society is made of people, and when individuals get rich and happy, society also gains. This is the so-called *Trickle Down Effect*. The rich can invest, start businesses, and employ people, innovate and market new products and goods, make profits, and the upward spiral of endless prosperity continues.

Anybody can become rich. There is equal opportunity for all. You have to have a dream and have to work hard at it to succeed. The *American Work Ethic* and the *Yankee Ingenuity* can overcome anything.

First, you have to be motivated and determined. You have to have a strong competitive or *killer* instinct to succeed. You should not be contented with what you have. That is, you should be greedy.

The system depends upon producing more goods at progressively lower cost to make more profit. However, it is never easy to get rich. More goods flooding the market means lower prices and lower profits. This is what the law of *Demand and Supply* is all about.

The trick is to make goods that don't last long. They should carry their own internal expiration date. That is called *Planned*

Obsolescence. That explains why our thirty-thousand dollar cars rust away in ten years, while a discarded empty can of Coke remains for ever.

To sustain such ever increasing production, one needs abundant natural resources to provide raw material and energy to run factories. Britain had to get these from its colonies, while America is blessed with inexhaustible natural resources.

Other costs are those related to personnel or Human Resources. America opted for industrialization over employing slave labor, and fought the Civil War over that. Industrialization and use of machines freed up the population from the drudgery and monotony of manual labor.

Mechanization offers other advantages like freedom from labor problems, and of workers' getting sick, disabled, or dying. Machines do not steal, do not complain, do not fight with one another, and can be recruited or idled at will. They do not need pensions either, and may be sold for scrap anytime.

Electronic revolution has fertilized this Garden of Eden still more. We do not need to describe the manifestations of the electronic revolution. If mechanical devices took over physical exertion, the electronic ones have liberated us from thinking, learning, reading and writing. That makes it practical for all of us to be literally tied down to our desks, desktops, and laptops without any visible chains from the rowing slaves.

Profit is determined by costs and sales price. Costs are incurred in procuring raw materials, energy—electric power, or manual labor, marketing, etc. Stated simply, material costs and personnel costs, since energy costs are largely fixed. Cost of raw materials can be lowered by exploiting other countries or having an abundant supply at home.

Selling goods at higher prices generates more profit, but it is not that easy. It may be difficult to agree on a fair price, but everybody recognizes the unfair price when one sees it. Capitalism depends upon free markets without any price controls, and the fair price is what the market will bear.

Open markets depend upon competition to control quality and prices. Therefore, the only way to increase profit is to promote products, overcome the competition, and increase *market share*. Having to pay lower taxes also raises profitability.

In this cutthroat environment, working efficiently is the key to success. Efficient utilization of resources translates into more profit. Survival of the fittest means only that of the efficient, nimble, lean and mean organization or business. Least amount of resources used for the least amount of time to produce maximum amount of goods or services is the game.

It seems to emerge that the only real cost-cutting is possible with personnel costs. These include salaries, fringe benefits like sick leave, vacation leave, Social Security and unemployment taxes, employer part of the health insurance premiums and pension plan contributions. Health insurance costs have been under severe scrutiny as the fastest growing and uncontrollable cost.

The easiest and the most effective way to cut personnel costs is to decrease the number of employees. All the costs listed above and the office costs decrease with fewer employees. Less office space, fewer computers, fewer phone lines, and less paper work add to the savings.

Merging of two or more companies can avoid duplication of services, and may allow trimming personnel costs. If two banks merge, few of their branches can be closed entirely. Letting some highly paid managerial workers go may generate more savings ("efficiency") while decreasing the numbers to be laid off, and its public relations aftershocks.

Generating more demand for goods requires advertising, marketing and promotion. These three are not identical but their purpose is the same, to increase demand. Open up newer designs, newer applications, make them easy to use, and make the consumer want to buy them rather than your appearing to push them. If there is a monopoly of sorts on a product, then decreasing its supply would increase profits for the company.

Larger companies and corporations are more successful in dealing with markets in the developing countries. A few of such corporations have more money than the budgets of those nations. They can offer financial incentives to those governments and their officials and in return, can secure better deals.

Running any business is a highly competitive endeavor. The world gets livable if interference from the government is kept to a minimum. Environmental and workplace safety regulations eat up lot of profit, by increasing the expense to meet them. Higher taxes can force employers to cut the work force to keep books balanced.

Businesses are in the business of making money for themselves, their partners, and shareholders. They cannot be expected to look after society, and its poor. Businesses create employment, provided the business is doing well. What is good for business is supposedly good for everybody.

This truth should always be the main principle of any capitalist economy. Any contrived job creation or protection of the poor is tantamount to practicing Socialism, or worse still, Communism. No American is expected to perpetrate that blasphemy!

4. WE, THE PEOPLE
AND OUR GOVERNMENT

Poor people and laborers are the rulers in Communism, so it is the rich who have to be concerned. Capitalists understandably hate Communism. Socialist governments look after the poor and not so poor people, and operate the essential services and businesses.

In the Capitalist system, the private sector resents the government's intruding into its domain, interfering with its running profitable agencies, and competing with it for precious dollars. It should be obvious that government should only be a not-for-profit entity.

There are other organizations that operate charities, and government should not levy tax on their inflow (shhh..don't call that *profit*). Just because they are not for profit, it does not mean that profits are not for them. The main point is, they do not pay taxes.

Business is not the only thing that is beyond any kind of meddling by government, Capitalism says, but religion and its organizations are also to be left alone. Religion and God are individual's absolutely personal matters, and hence the *separation of the State and the Church* is sacrosanct.

Again, that does not prevent the church from interfering in, manipulating, and practically commandeering the State. Thank God, they are not levying taxes on the government, not yet, anyway.

Healthcare business is a noble endeavor and hospitals cannot be taxed. Moreover, the government should give them grant money to further the cause of medicine without sacrificing their own.

Hospitals receive endowments and still depend upon services of its volunteer corps to sustain humanity, and they reward high school volunteers by facilitating their admittance to better colleges, in return for their volunteering. They may also get services from interns, residents, and other house-staff at a highly discounted rate to survive.

Other professional bodies demand similar unpaid apprenticeship before admitting the new members into their folds. This is of course, strictly voluntary and is meant to protect the professional standards and public at large from incompetents. Making money calls for highly competent people.

Now we are entering murky waters. It seems that our financial house is divided against itself, and is struggling to stand. We are a nation of entrepreneurs, highly motivated, hard working, and dedicated group of workaholics, with a good business aptitude and risk tolerance. Those who are owners of private businesses are apparently more American than the rest of us mortals.

Our idea of freedom and independence is so ingrained in our psyche that a mere thought of working for someone else conjures up images of impotence on one hand, and of slavery on the other.

Ben Franklin unwittingly furthered their cause by saying, "Those who give up liberty for a little safety, deserve neither liberty nor safety!" They should be subservient to the *real* Americans, and their businesses.

We are in the land of equal opportunity for being broke or unemployed. Businesses cannot hire you if their sales are down and payrolls are up. Then you start collecting unemployment insurance paid for by your now ex-employer. Moreover, you begin to bite away chunks of money from the pool which is supposed to help out businesses, should the need arise.

All love triangles are strange, but none as strange the one among people, government, and business. The government is of the people, who are in turn, employees of business, which in turn feeds on the government. What happens when people are not employed by business, or are not running their own business? They work for the local, state, and federal governments and thereby competing with business.

That puts business and government at odds with each other, and people into no man's land between them. It takes money, lot of it, to create jobs. *Productive* jobs (created by the industry) pay for themselves in increased revenue and profit. *Jobs as relief* programs (operated by the government) are just expensive, we are informed.

Government does not always have the money but it can theoretically generate it by levying taxes or by selling treasury bills or by simply printing it. Employed workers pay taxes and make purchases. They buy cars and houses, make mortgage payments, and send kids to summer camps.

They also pay back their own students' college loans. The least the employed do is to stop collecting the unemployment benefit. All these activities produce income for the government, and sales for business.

On the other hand, one unemployed person effectively removes at least 10 consumers from the market. His or her family, friends and colleagues stop making major and then minor purchases.

There is nothing mystical about bringing consumers back to the markets. They are not made in some factory, or maybe, they indeed are, but in a different way. One company's employees are consumers of another company, and the other way around.

People as employees generate products, and as consumers they buy them. In doing so, they generate taxes, and pay income and Social Security taxes, and pay their health insurance premiums to make business, governments, and society continue to function.

5. THE MATING BEHAVIOR
OF THE PRAYING MANTIS

Capitalism is a marvelous system and it has served America well for over two centuries. It is still functioning reasonably well and is producing wealth for us. There is no dearth of money. We still give foreign aid, conduct one or more wars, and help those distressed by natural and other calamities.

For the last few years, especially after the attacks on the twin towers of the World Trade Center, the American spirit has given way to despair and gloom. Suddenly we have begun to feel poor, not a healthy feeling for anyone, certainly not for one of the richest and powerful nations like America.

"In God we trust," and these are definitely the times to pray, even though we are not on our knees yet, and hope never to be. Lowly creatures like the mantis also appear to pray. In the premed years, in our Biology class we first read about these fascinating creatures, and subsequently read more about them in the Natural History and other magazines.

Mating habits of animals and creatures of all sizes and shapes are fascinating to all minds young and old. Quirkiness of the mating behavior of the black *widow* spider is known quite well. That of the praying mantis is equally quirky, made more intriguing by its lack of strong scientific verification, thereby making it a suitable metaphor for our present narration.

We, the people, man and women alike, are feeling that we are the male praying mantis. The latter finds the object of his desire, and mounts on top of her in an amorous embrace. He reaches out, or rather in, and begins to make deposit of his masculine wealth.

His partner turns her head around with lust and a salivating mouth, reaches for and grabs his head between her front legs, and plants on it a kiss of death, biting it off, and eating it away.

Even devoid of his head or maybe, because of it, the male loses all his inhibitions and with more vigorous love making, keeps making his deposit with increasing interest. Nothing can be accomplished without putting oneself into it.

Almost the entire male body soon ends up being in the female stomach, yes, stomach, not just the belly. Only the male organ and its system still continue to work. The cannibal copulation concludes with only the wings being left. Wings are the stuff of our dreams.

Our system works, and our dreams endure, remaining just that.

Don't start blaming the females of any species. All creatures, including humans will ignore any danger to complete the sex act. Even without the female literally eating up the head, the latter can be very easily lost to our greed and other base instincts.

In the remaining pages we will see how our financial intercourse is progressing and why we find ourselves in the predicament in which we have landed naively, and possibly try to extricate ourselves.

6. CAPITALISM
IN THE POSTCOLONIAL ERA

We do not replace things just because they are old. Newer things may be far advanced technologically, they may be more shapely, and of course, of the latest fashion, but we like to hold on to things until they become totally useless, and even dangerous. Although Capitalism advocates planned obsolescence for manufactured goods, its own exhausted relevance may not be easy to contemplate.

Old, it certainly is. India's prime Minister Nehru used to say, "I often wonder whether the ability to survive is, in itself, necessarily a good thing." Maybe not, but Capitalism has served us well, and it is still working. The latter itself could be a problem. If the engine of a capsized boat continues to run, the boat can move far away from its passenger, leaving the latter on the high seas.

Any system that we adopt has to be in our own interest at the least. Capitalism has seen us to the top of our riches. England amassed its wealth by sucking its colonies dry. America did not have to do that. Its resources were abundant, and its growing population provided an ever expanding market. One would really have to be an incurable cynic to find fault with that, however, find faults we must, at least try to.

Simply stated, instead of exploiting colonies, *we were, and have been exploiting ourselves,* which is not a crime in itself. One segment of our country was getting richer at the expense of the other. Nobody was doing anything wrong. It is just that we have been unable to see what has not been right with it all along.

In my younger days, I remember reading about a stray dog that was starving, when it found a dried up bone, and started licking and biting it. There was nothing to eat in that. He kept on biting harder until one of its own teeth came loose and began to bleed. Taste of blood encouraged him to bite deeper, with more blood oozing out. Such are our successes. We are savoring our own blood.

We still have lot more resources, but they are being depleted, and may soon be exhausted, if we do not protect them from squandering. From the thirteen colonies on the east coast, we have expanded *from the sea to shining sea,* and beyond to Hawaii and Alaska.

All that space is being filled with people having their own dreams, and we are in a *zero-*

sum game now, in which, if one wins, the other has to lose. If I eat, you cannot. If I get rich, you will become poor. Our riches have become the cause of our poverty.

It is the same system, but the situation has changed, affecting results adversely. In the years before the Civil War, we managed to get slave labor from the "colonies" in Africa. The emancipation of slaves established our preference for the machines and other technology to come. We chose to remove "human" from human resources.

While liberating the imported slaves from their bondage, we also sowed the seeds for idling the native workers in the future, and that future has caught up with us. Machines increase production, increase efficiency, raise the profits, and may simultaneously increase unemployment as well.

Machines were supposed to be saving us from the monotonous and repetitive drudgery and from heavy tasks, while providing us with more leisure and free time from work, but they have ended up freeing us from all work. One person can use a machine to replace 15 workers, but another machine can replace all 16 workers as well, we failed to notice.

True, "Guns don't kill, people do." Machines do not layoff or fire people, people do. However, people are not likely to stop laying others off, if doing so is going to decrease their profits. Unemployment is the price we pay for our greed for profits.

Needs of one are sacrificed to protect the wants of another. This should have bothered somebody's conscience, but let's not get sentimental, this is serious business.

This may sound like a call to arms for class warfare, but it is not. Since rich can become poor, and vice versa, there is only one class here, with its two aspects. If we can refrain from having different set of standards for each phase that we might be in at one moment, we should be able to find our way out of this morass. Which morass? Umm...let's see.

7. CAR WITH A STUCK GAS PADDLE

Business would want the government to stay out of meddling in its pursuit of profit. That is like removing the brakes or having a stuck accelerator. If the rich are getting richer at the expense of the poor getting poorer, so be it.

Big government can really act like the big brother. It can watch and scrutinize use of resources, disposal of pollutants, safety of employees and of products for those who are to use them, and of the environment. It can set standards and implement regulations as required. Worse still, it can impose taxes and penalties.

Understandably, business does not like a big and strong government like the proverbial 600 pound gorilla. Anything that the government does, cuts into profits. Value of a business does not yet depend upon the number of trees saved, or barrels of oil not used, or the number of kids who did not die of lead poisoning. In military terms, all that is *collateral damage*, and is to be accepted calmly.

Business is the only entity that can employ people productively, or so it claims. However, it does not consider it to be its duty to create and provide jobs. Nor is it its responsibility to ensure the safety of the workplace to protect them. People should earn their jobs. They should be prudent, careful, and smart enough to look out for themselves. Hiring them is costing enough.

Industrial and electronic revolutions have largely spared business that agony as well. Machines can do their work, and computer can enable companies get by with fewer employees.

In many big factories, robots have all but replaced human beings, for people's own good and safety. Incidences of on the job injuries have plummeted, and compensation cases have been minimized.

All this is good for profit, the latter is good for business and its owners. In addition, profit is profitable. It increases the value of the company's stock on Wall Street, since a company's *market valuation* depends upon number of shares outstanding, and their street price. Higher valuation tends to raise the stock price further.

Therefore, it is good to keep the government away. A smaller and preferably weaker government, deprived of the means to hire inspectors to find violations can let the companies be more valuable. Government should have barely adequate funds to mind its own business, which is, nothing. That should require no funds.

Government should not run any profitable business. The private sector can do that better. If not the entire enterprise, at least the profitable parts of it can be operated by private companies. For example, FedEx can deliver letters better than the US Mail. The United Parcel Service (UPS) can do the same with packages and parcels.

FedEx and UPS can charge for Saturday delivery or that to a residence, while the Postal Service has been doing both for free, even while losing money. We merrily pay the private companies for the extras that were supposed to be free to begin with. How come we are so reluctant to pay our own government?

If the government-operated hospitals treat patients who have ample health insurance, they can take away a sizable chunk of business from private hospitals. Making profit is not a prerogative of the government. That is what business is for.

Government-run ventures are supposedly poorly managed and inefficiently run. They mostly lose money, require subsidies and cost the tax payers dearly. Government offices are staffed, we are told, by poorly motivated and lazy employees supposedly unfit for any employment. I wonder, why?

If the private sector takes away lucrative businesses, services and skilled employees using its financial might, government has to make do with the leftover crumbs. I know, I have been there and I have been that. Let me say it right now, and right here, that nobody works as hard under as much adversity as the government employees, and with as much dedication despite the negative and punitive rewards system.

If a city hospital in New York gets $450 a day per patient treated to cover all costs incurred, a private hospital will get $700, plus charges for lab, x-rays, and medicines. Moreover, doctors will bill separately for their services, and consultants will bill still more. Their total will be close to one thousand dollars a day for the same services. But, private hospitals provide better care. Any wonder they do, at two and a half times the going rate?

It is not to be construed that business is totally against any kind of interference by the government. The latter ought to be there to use its muscle should the Chinese dump their goods on America, or the Japanese cars flood our markets.

It should be there to prevent migrant workers from (ab)using our facilities and educational and health services. It should stop the invasion by alien doctors like myself by denying them the visa.

Most important, should big business get into trouble, get broke of its own doing, and may need to be bailed out, the government should be standing on alert with all its resources and might which it was not supposed to have had in first place. Don't you think this is a bit too complicated?

8. RIDING THE BRAKES

Lately one is given the impression that our businesses, large and small are paralyzed by stifling government regulations and demanding fuel-efficiency standards. Our businesses are being taxed into oblivion, while China, Japan, Korea, and other countries, supported by their governments are driving us out of our own markets.

That is how business feels, and we have to be sensitive to its feelings. If one is awaiting the arrival of utopia with no restrictions of any kind and no hindrance to unlimited profits, any and every little traffic sign may generate a panic attack. For those of you who are not doctors, I should inform you that in medicine, *panic* means severe anxiety *for which there is no discernible reason*.

Total or partial control of industries and resources by the state is the characteristic of Socialism and Communism, and no one has claimed yet that we are already there. The rich and powerful (redundant use of words) have successfully resisted higher taxes for themselves. That includes income tax, capital gains tax, and estate tax, to name a few.

On the other hand, the Social Security tax has been increasing steadily. Mostly the poor pay them, because the taxable amount is capped, and the rich do not pay more than a "rich" poor man. Also remember, it is a tax on money that one has not even received yet.

Of course, employers pay 50% of it. However, they pay it from money they have earned and pocketed, and they do get a tax deduction, unlike their employees. The Social Security tax not only does not hurt the employers as much as it does to its employees. Rumors of the sky falling down are premature.

New drivers and other insecure drivers tend to ride the brakes. They press the gas paddle to get going, but are afraid to pick up speed. So, they put the other foot on the brakes at the same time. This slows the car and wastes gas, but keeps it moving anyway. Sometimes that is what we may really need to do, for example, passing through a deep puddle of water, or when we are in deep waters, as we find ourselves in today.

Our federal government has been weakened enough. Although it has been able to achieve stellar successes in offshore wars, it has been stymied by party politics to achieve anything for the masses. Having bailed out the banks, the car companies, solar energy ventures, and insurance companies, it finds itself unable to create jobs for almost 10% of the workforce, idled for more than a year.

Our brakes are jammed. We need to ride the brakes for a while. Business is shooting itself in the foot by not creating jobs and starting to hire. Their attitude is that of the proverbial husband who would not mind even dying, if he could make his wife a widow!

Recovery is almost here, but it cannot be sustained unless the consumers start buying. The newly homeless, unemployed, and uninsured are not going to rush to the shopping malls to rescue the sinking economy. Business cannot create jobs if there is no demand for its products, and demand cannot come without employment. This is what is called long term approach, an endless one at that.

9. *FROM UNDER THE KNIFE IN THE COLONIES*

No one in the U.S.A. can claim to have lived during the colonial period. The latter has become a reason for celebration of our successful liberation from the British rule. We go to colonial Williamsberg, and Jamestown, and other places to celebrate the American history, and the spirit that prevailed then.

I have had a chance to be born in and spend first few years of my life in colonial India under the same British rule. Not that I remember much from my firsthand observations, but I had ample chance to study the effects of colonialism on my country of birth, in my high school history classes.

The Gandhian literature told me a lot about effects of colonialism in other parts of Asia, and of Africa, especially South Africa. India was colonized to further the trade, and later to spread the Christianity. In that fashion, a country can be enslaved, and be offered its salvation simultaneously.

Indian tea resulted in the Boston Tea Party in the colonial America, while India had to await its own Salt March to come 150 years later. General Cornwallis organized the British rule in India, after surrendering to George Washington at Yorktown.

Colonization breeds violence, wars, and dictatorships. It can thwart democracy. Dukes and chieftains can be bought over or conquered and manipulated. Colonies' raw materials can be carted away, processed, and more expensive goods can be dumped on it. Locally produced merchandize can be heavily taxed into their demise.

If colonial governance is not taken over formally, its officers can be coerced or bribed into submission. Those officers can be effectively turned into string puppets. Skilled labor of the colony can be destroyed, and imported machined products can be glamorized.

Colonial cheap labor can be exploited to transport the goods in the wrong direction. Colonies can be gently *persuaded* into buying worthless, useless, and outright harmful imported products. They can be divided and weapons of attacks and of defense both can be sold to both sides. Opium from India could be forcibly sold to China by the British, extracting obscene profit along the way.

Worst of all, colonies are stripped of their culture, religion, social customs, traditions, pride, honor, and even self respect. Today, there are no colonial powers like that, but we have their modern *avatars*.

Mighty multinationals with their budgets bigger than the entire national budgetary outlays can get whatever they want. They can create their own homemade utopia of operating with impunity without any hindrance from anyone, and often being thanked in return for the modernization instead. Only if our own government would be so thankful!

Our companies believe in *point of service* care. They use raw material from the modern day financial colonies, purchased at dirt cheap prices having bribed the officers, use readily available, eager to work labor under any kind of work environment, to produce their wares at nominal cost, ensuring greater profit. So far so good. American people reap the benefits.

10. THE COLONIZATION OF AMERICA

In old days, exploiting the colonies benefitted the motherland, and with the modern financial colonies, it still remains true. Unlike the older times, this modern colonization can hurt the motherland as well.

When the US went to war with Iraq to protect the oil flow from the ulterior aims of Saddam Hussein, we had to protect and secure the free flow of oil to our shores. Leaving aside the entire issue of dependence on foreign oil, it was feared that muzzling that spigot could seriously impair our manufacturing and other commerce.

The US achieved its goals and the war ended with our success, or so we thought. The prices at the gas pump reached an unprecedented high, far higher than what the infamous dictator would ever have been able to achieve. Our father and son Presidents, and the vice president all happened to be owners of oil companies, and were *unable* to control the price hike.

So, the idea was to protect the prices, and not the supplies of oil. The intention was to control the inflow of oil all along. We sure needed the *regime change!* This is the stuff future recessions are made of.

Our companies working abroad in sheer disregard for any regulations, can bring back goods that are manufactured without an iota of thought about their quality and safety. It may be years before these problems can be discovered.

Multinational corporations can move their incomes abroad where they can extract favorable tax exemptions, and avoid paying any tax at all in the US. What may be called tax cheating should you and I commit that, gives an upper hand to these companies.

They can negotiate an amnesty with the US government, to bring home some of that money without paying any tax or penalty. Who says that the Internal Revenue Service has no heart! Corporations vaguely offer to create jobs in the US with that money, and the people and the government of the USA should be eternally grateful for that.

Manufacturing goods abroad with cheaper raw materials may help the mother country, but that moves the jobs abroad, creating unemployment at home. Remember, business cannot be encumbered with moral considerations. Their duty is to produce the merchandize at the lowest possible cost to the companies that have to swallow the concomitant higher profits.

Wait, that's not all. When the goods are manufactured continents away from here, we end up importing them. In essence, we export our jobs, lose the revenue from tax on business and on wages, gain no money at all, and import readymade goods. Isn't that exactly what happened to the colonies?

Moreover, these imported goods tilt the balance of trade adversely. Our own companies export goods to us, and increase our trade deficit. With such benevolent friends, why can't we be a bit appreciative?

Unemployment is our problem, not theirs. Corporations have lot of ingenuity and can convert any problem into an opportunity to make more money. That is called business acumen. Unemployment keeps inflation under control, and it can be used to keep the labor unions on a short leash also. The unions feel compelled to accept lower wages and benefits for their membership to hang on to its precious jobs.

Business is not expected to create jobs, it can always export the jobs abroad, and it does not need the native expensive workers. It wants consumers, not employees. Who can tell them that the two are the same!

11. LIFE IN THE COLONY AT HOME

Although America has had been a British colony, it did not have to suffer as much as counterparts in Asia and Africa. That deprivation has been more than made up for thanks to our own corporations, untouchable by taxes.

If these businesses have larger budgets than some other countries, very few of them can come close to that of the US government. Local, state, and county governments are within easier reach. At federal level also, individual legislators need money for their elections and reelections. The President needs that far more. Not only they are not all saints, some are in it just for the sin.

Businesses can exact favorable tax treatments, subsidies, grants, and desired legislation in return for their support. Many of these, while helpful to donors, may be detrimental to the taxpayers and the country at large.

Legislative actions thus generated may encourage waste, pollution of the environment, and may block creation of alternate sources of energy. Worse, such influence may make elected officers oblivious to the public interest and opinion.

Agreed that money has always influenced political activity, and it always will. However, some semblance of decency is not too much to ask for. Lobbyists for gun dealers, farmers, tobacco companies, religious groups, the American Medical Association, AARP, and many others are highly influential.

We can live with the above as a fact of life. When potential candidates for the Presidency can start taking pledges to oppose or support one or another lobby, that speaks for the sad colonization of the USA, the *land of the free and the home of the brave*.

A confused group of politicians unable to address the unemployment, homelessness, foreclosures, recession, healthcare, or any such things vying to appease one or the other vote bank is an ultimate disgrace.

There is nothing anti-anything in the above. It is about restoring the American dignity and self respect, while pointing it out that still there are American people, and that they should matter. America should honor its commitments to its allies.

Recent reports about President Obama's being sufficiently pro-Israel or otherwise made someone run a daily report card and a meter of sort on the front page of the internet edition of the New York Times.

That was accompanied by the ex-mayor, late Mr. Koch of New York proclaiming frequently his daily index of whether, based on the above, he would campaign for or against Mr. Obama. This is not freedom of speech, it is simply arrogance.

At least those of us who were naturalized to the citizenship of the USA, had to declare on solemn affirmation our giving up all loyalty and commitment to another country, no matter how friendly it may be. Maybe, citizens by birth are exempt from unwavering loyalty to America. I am sure, nobody would want to have solid support from a weak and humiliated ally.

As for the religious right, is it conceivable that this nation of ours cannot produce one Galileo or one Martin Luther (not King, Jr.)? One thousand goats make a lion not. Getting elected or reelected is important, but should not our officers be doing something beyond that?

Jefferson was always fighting "against any kind of tyranny over the minds of men." Colonial transformation of our mindset is the worst kind of tyranny, especially so, because it is inflicted upon us, by supposedly our own.

☆ ☆ ☆

12. GREED, INC.

In greed we trust, far more than in God. You can speak against the latter invoking your right to free speech. However, exercising that against the former can be very unwise. Without greed, there will be stagnation of profit, and loss of competitive edge. Profit should always increase.

Profit is the difference between costs and sales. Decreasing the cost of production is the first step. Once raw materials are procured, factory is set up, and energy supply is assured, efficiency and skill of the work force become important.

Efficiency is the key word in today's business. You may call it *productivity* also. To produce goods in the cheapest way is the aim. Getting employees to work at lower pay, without benefits, for longer hours, and on weekends can boost the bottom line. By threatening labor unions with unemployment, these can be extracted.

The best way to lower personnel costs is to have fewer people working. It is not enough to spare the businesses the agony of creating jobs, we should sympathize with their need and fiscal mandate to eliminate them. Businesses love the humanity as their potential customers, but they abhor the mere thought of hiring people and ruin the profits.

One can always do a little more, and good managers can certainly tap that potential of the remaining staff effectively. If the staff does not like that, they can certainly quit. Businesses can easily replace them by hiring someone else, but why would they? The ex-colleagues can pick up the slack created. That is how companies become lean and mean.

Employees remaining behind should prove to the bosses that they are up to par to meet new challenges and to handle any crises. If they do not get totally crushed, they can aspire to get a raise or bonus that, it so happens, is reserved for the managers who worked so hard to keep the workers employed and busy.

One can wait for a while, survive couple of more challenges, and then finally decide to follow in the footsteps of one's departed colleague, leading to the door. Every such small step by every employee is a giant step for the managers to increase the efficiency. Their bonuses increase still more. Layoff one hundred employee and promote one. That's efficiency. What is their efficiency, is our unemployment.

It is attractive to cut down research activity, and to close the library. The former eats away money, and the latter has no obvious relevance to generating profits. Research requires pouring money down the drain with no immediate payoff. It is far more tempting to tinker with existing products, make some minor changes here and there, and come up with new and improved ones.

Closing the research department means losing the tax write off. It is better to undermine it, fund it poorly, and equip it in such a way that nothing of any substance can ever come out of it. Understaffing the research department makes it more efficient at producing nothing.

Companies cannot be bothered with conserving resources. Recycling raw material is cumbersome, but if the consumer sentiment is in its favor, let the marketing department start claiming and bragging about the recycling initiatives, charging consumers to pick up their carefully saved and collected recyclables, and punish the municipalities for their indiscretion shown by implementing such programs.

Customers are encouraged to take the lead to protect the environment by opting for paperless billing. That saves the company lot of paper, and postage. These can be effectively used to send more daily promotional material stuffed in massive envelops. Billing is so counterproductive.

You and I would stupidly lower the asking price of our used car or house if it fails to sell. Our car companies raised the prices of their new large gas guzzler cars to compete with the fuel efficient and smaller Japanese cars. Increasing the sales is plain silly, it is the profit, stupid! Loyal customers would merrily pay more out of love and patriotism.

Companies manufacture four or five versions of the same product with slight differences. However they all come with the same instruction sheet or operating manual, and it is up to the consumer to figure out which diagrams apply to his or her purchase. If a company can produce five products to please its buyers, how can it afford to print so many manuals?

13. DAWN OF ANTI-CONSUMERISM

We have heard a lot about not biting the hand that feeds one, or about killing the golden-egg-laying hen. For the corporate conquistadors, the subjects of the colony are to be sucked dry of all wealth that can be squeezed out, but without killing them.

It is the duty of those poor souls to patronize their masters, patriotically keep their bottomless pockets overflowing, and yet be proud of the unmitigated success of our Capitalist system.

Customer service is what the customers are supposed to provide by purchasing merchandize. Staffing the service desk also requires hiring personnel at the cost of profits. Putting some naive, inexperienced employee to occupy that chair is enough to keep customers from demanding too much.

Customer has to be satisfied, and surveys of their opinions should express their delight on a scale of 1-10. Customer's phone calls are so invaluable that the customers are always put on hold for hours at a time.

Public opinion is the guiding light for any business. Giving the public what it wants, or giving the nation what it needs is difficult, but marketing departments are smart enough to make the consumers, customers, and people at large feel that companies are always doing just what is the best thing to do, in the cheapest way, without doing anything at all.

Progress and industrialization as were once seen in photographs of chimneys billowing smoke, environmental friendliness as shown by a pair of pristine white swans gracefully gliding away on emerald waters into the sunset, cigarettes symbolizing manhood, can pull wool over any casual eye.

There are bandwagons of environment, recycling, customer satisfaction, high quality at low price, educated consumer being the best customer, and of course of putting you first into whatever.

Sales circulars carry lot of coupons, offer discounts, and dangle rebates in front of our eyes. Government rebates and tax credits are the surest lures. Whether one buys windows or central air conditioning while they are still under rebates or tax credits, or does so a few days after they expire, one pays the same amount of money.

Rebates and tax credits are to stimulate consumer purchases of energy efficient materials and devices. However, companies have better use for that money. Incentives given to consumers are wasted, while companies are better placed and able to use them to increase their profits, and market valuations.

The creature called customer is so gullible that (s)he can be easily deceived by selling him or her 14 oz of cereal in a one pound (16 oz) box. Selling packages of eleven bananas rather than a dozen is a smart move. Prestigious magazines sell an annual subscription covering all eleven issues, not twelve.

Have you tried to buy larger sizes to save money? A one pound package does not necessarily sell for less than four packages of a quarter pound each. Products without any real competitive marketplace are conducive of highway robberies by retailers. Look at dentures, dental implants, orthodontics, hearing aids, and plastic surgery.

Not only the customers, but products can be treated like orphans. Life-saving or preserving drugs for an uncommon disease may be glamorous, but are profitable in very small way. Producing them can be abandoned or held hostage to extract some other concession from the government. The latter is known as *maximization* or it is discreetly described as *optimization*.

If a big government collecting heavy taxes is not welcome, a starving and hence, thrifty one trying to save money is not desirable either. Any attempt to reduce payments by Medicare or Medicaid for medical office care or prescription items generates dire predictions of playing with quality of patient care.

The best and the most embarrassing example of such an uproar was the slandering of foreign doctors providing care to poor patients in ghetto areas, by the medical establishment trying to protect a high standard of living for their membership. None of the latter would be willing to even venture into those inner city areas.

One good thing did come out of that commotion though. Public found out that it is possible for doctors to be bad, too. Regulations were introduced to monitor patient care, and an explosion of malpractice suits followed. Foreign doctors were not found to be any worse than the presumed best quality natives.

Now we are hearing a lot about shortage of nurses. It would not be long before some wasted interest starts crying over the supposedly poor quality of foreign nurses, their inability to be sensitive to comfort our patients, worsened by their limited familiarity with our languages, conveniently ignoring the obvious that these patients are suffering without any nurses.

Language is not a bad weapon either, in fighting for the bottom lines. I know someone born and brought up in the US, who had done an M.S. in Biology from the New York University. That student had to clear the TOEFL (Test Of English as a Foreign Language) before being permitted to take the medical licensing exam (USMLE) after becoming a doctor from a Caribbean med school!

Medicare and Medicaid are blamed as being wasteful on one hand, and being stingy with payments to doctors, etc., on another. Once these programs start paying for something, the businesses start pushing their customers to apply for them. Wheelchairs, blood sugar meters, hospital beds for home use, motorized scooters, all are advertised on TV, with statements like, "No cost to you," "We'll do all paperwork," and so on. It is hoped that these government programs would not offer mercy killing.

We have to be self sufficient in producing the essential labor force like doctors, nurses, and farm hands on our own. We need migrant farm workers, but treat them like criminals, and deprive them of basic educational and medical services. Our half hearted and ambivalent approach creates unbearable misery for some.

There are so many professional interns, externs, apprentices, research assistants, clerks, and what not, working without any pay or with pittance, under the guise of training and experience. Many a time, there is no one around to be doing that training. It is organized bullying and hazing.

We do not ask our elected legislators to work without pay for the first year of their term. However, our businesses and professional bodies have managed to, more than make up for the slave labor banned by President Lincoln.

Moreover, many employees are made middle managers in name and titles only, without giving them any authority to hire and fire. They sit in the executive meetings without any power to make policy decisions. These managers work overtime, including on weekends, without receiving a single extra penny, just because they are called *managers*. Can't call them *bonded slaves,* because that would be too honest.

High school students are supposed to work in the neighborhood hospitals to show their community spirit, and thereby make their college applications more impressive. Most hospitals do the preliminary health checkups and administer necessary vaccinations to them as a courtesy, while some prestigious ones charge the volunteers for these.

Just because it is called *voluntary*, it does not become so, nor does it cease to be slavery either. Taking undue advantage of altruistic volunteers is unconscionable, and for anybody to profit from them is a sin.

If someone gains something, they should pay for it. Rather than paying these poor, desperate, unemployed workers, providing free services for altruistic reasons, or for improving their own chances of getting accepted by a good college, or getting hired by the same authority, some employers are even charging them fees to provide the privilege of working for free in a noble pursuit. Shame is too inadequate a term to describe this.

14. OUR FRIENDLY NEIGHBORHOOD BANK

The only image that comes to mind on thinking about our neighborhood bank, is a giant vacuum cleaner, suctioning off all our hard earned money mercilessly and without causing any obvious pain to us. It then lends money to local businesses, keeps neighborhoods thriving, and advances all of us enough money for us to chase our great American dream of owning a house.

It is almost un-American to rent a house, it seems. Renters do not get any tax breaks, or a tax shelter. Their rent money just vanishes, without providing any ownership of real estate. Owning a house gives you all that, and makes you the owner of a real estate which keeps on increasing its value, that is, it *appreciates*.

The house forces you to save money regularly and pay it to the bank. In turn you build property right or *owner's equity*. The bank also gives us credit cards to let us pay for what we need and want, without being in any hurry to pay it back.

Scarcely do we realize that instead of renting a living place, we are renting money. Instead of heating up and cooling a small place, we have a larger one to contend with, and have to illuminate it inside and around it. It stimulates our greed to take out the equity and put it in high rewards and high risk instruments. We may end up losing our shelter, as many have recently found out, and our shirts as well.

We cannot blame the bank for our own greed, but they have their own, too. Bank exacts fees for anything one can think of, and more. It can withhold your cleared check for a couple of days extra to make money on it. That's called, collecting *spread*.

Use of automatic teller machines (ATM), seeing a living teller, bounced checks, debit card transactions, foreign transactions, over use and nonuse penalties, fees for failing to maintain a certain minimum balance, and many more fees can eat away lot of your dough.

Recent follies by banks like *sub-prime mortgages*, hasty foreclosures, improper documentation, do not have to be enumerated here. Their multibillion dollar bailout by the federal government, without getting any control over the banks is the latest testament to their power.

Despite the stern warning from the feds, banks had no qualms about giving hefty bonuses to their CEOs (Chief Executive Officer), bonuses unabashedly described as being *contractual*. None of the CEOs was fired for mismanaging funds and for exercising poor judgment, if any at all.

In a fantastic quirk of financial logic, we were informed that those CEOs were the only ones skilled and knowledgeable enough to guide the banks out of the mess they had created, and hence deserved to be paid a premium over their salaries.

I wish we doctors could obtain malpractice reforms like that. Let me explain. Suppose I operated upon you to remove your appendix, and left a forceps in your belly, by mistake. You developed a bad peritonitis.

Now, since I am the only one who really knows where that forceps is, and am in position to take it out, I can call without any shame, your health insurance carrier to pay me one and a half times the usual fee for an appendectomy! What is so difficult about it?

Banks blackmailed the feds into bailing them out, holding the entire credit market and the entire country hostage, declaring themselves to be too big to fail. Now they are trying for an encore performance in Europe on the issue of helping out Greece. Banks want all their money to be safely returned before saving Greece, or else!

You have to be a financial wizard to run a bank. Best brains coming out of our prestigious business schools are recruited to manage those. Under their watchful eyes, banks collect your money practically free of interest, because it is safer in their hands than under your pillow.

You can borrow that money back for your home mortgage at 5% interest, or for financing your new car for 10%. If you are your bank's favorite customer who enjoys carrying a large balance on credit cards, the bank rewards your loyalty by charging you 25-30% interest. When is the last time you saw a shark wearing a three piece suit?

This way of making money is called business, and has been around for millennia. Anybody can do that. However, then there are things only a genius can do. Can you come up with a possible way having borrowed the money at no interest, lending it at 30%, and yet, managing to go broke, requiring a bailout?

Do you think, if we had put some monkeys instead, to run these banks, would they have done any worse? Why don't we lock up our business schools and save the tuition money of parents of these promising business school graduates!

15. THE WALL STREET

Wall Street is not the place one should want to occupy. It is unnecessarily and undeservedly getting the bad rap lately. True, it is the haunted house of financial horrors, where you can meet the beauty, as well as the beast. However, it is not fair to blame an innocent street for our own untamed collective greed.

Wall Street or the stock market does not want to move up or down or sideways. Rather, our aggregate wishful thinking moves it. The stock market is nothing more than a place where one can buy or sell a partnership stake in one or more of innumerable companies listed there. Many of us gamble there by placing bets on predicted value of a company, just like betting on the outcome of a cricket or a soccer match.

Many claims are made for America being a land of this or that. Equality is among the foremost among them. Wall Street is the only and truly well documented equal opportunity institution, providing everybody a fair chance of going broke. It has many agents aptly called, *brokers* to guide you in that, albeit for a fee.

The street does have a strange personality, and nobody has been able to figure it out, except to discover the impossibility of accomplishing that task. Many rich doctors also frequent it, and maybe, that is how it has acquired the tradition of considering all good things as negative, and bad ones as positive. If your test for any disease is positive, you have it, and vice versa.

If the unemployment decreases, the Street hates it. The Street cheers its rise and consequent hope of less inflation. If a company declares that it had a profitable year, Wall Street sheds tears on that profit being relatively less, or on a likely slower next year. When you expect it to plummet on some long awaited bad news, it ignores the latter as something it has already figured in.

Nobody is smart enough to outsmart the Street for too long. Therefore, the smart ones invest someone else's money and take a cut. Whatever reality there is, is too distorted to be believed or described.

Although Wall Street does not commit any crime, those who do, practice their art there. It is like an ongoing ballroom dance, where everybody wants to project an image of themselves which has nothing to do with reality. It is a hall of mirrors of sorts. We visit it for the fun, which comes at our expense anyway.

Wall Street is not just a street, nor just a building on it, but rather our concerted subconscious and highly biased opinion about one or more companies listed there, based on what the latters tell us about themselves.

What they do tell us is generally only what they want to tell us, guided by what we like to hear and believe, no matter how implausible that may be. Neither of us goes there searching for truth.

Companies want to appear sexier than what they are, with lot of reinforcing padding in appropriate places, and we cherish the sight. Augmentation by plastic surgery is more effective than flimsy pads. It is nothing less or more than a mating dance, of the praying mantis, though.

Companies can exaggerate their projected profits, but that does not work for long. The boost has to be real, just as all illusions are. Companies do their best to make as much profit as they can by reducing costs and increasing their sales and profit margins, and shedding the tax burden. Now that cake needs some icing.

Having controlled the factors that can be, there is still one item left that can be cut, and that is, personnel cost. It is one item that the CEOs can manipulate skillfully to achieve the maximum efficiency. To achieve the same level of profits with the lowest payroll is the key.

Increasing sales or decreasing other costs is not always feasible beyond a certain limit, but cutting the personnel contingent is always possible, even in a company with a bare bone staffing level. Payroll cuts immediately show up as increased profits, measure for measure. Projected liabilities related to pension and healthcare outlays are also lowered in turn.

Replacing human beings with machines can make it possible to produce everything with no personnel expense, but that requires huge initial investment of the capital. It is more economical to replace the laid off personnel by overworking the rest.

We chase the stocks of such highly profitable companies, pushing up their prices and market valuations. The CEOs receive obscene bonuses for achieving efficiency by trimming the fat. Should the remaining employees start complaining, letting them go can boost the success infinitely. Forget the old fashioned product improvement, quality control, and customer satisfaction; these are irrelevant.

Creativity resides in improving the profits without improving the sales or the profit margins, or any such cumbersome and unreliable drudgery. Companies can keep on shrinking, their sales dwindle, product lines dry up, customer base and its satisfaction get eroded, and its CEOs get rewarded for achieving all that. What are a few million jobs on the altar of efficiency and growth on Wall Street!

This game is aptly called, convincing Wall Street, or simply, *convincing the markets*. No need to convince Main Street, because Wall Street is the main and the only street that matters.

16. PROTECTING
THE CASTLES IN THE AIR

As the joke goes, a neurotic is a person who builds castles in the air, a psychotic lives in that, while the psychiatrist is the one who collects the rent. Our castles in the air may not be real, but they truly need to be guarded. No discussion of truth and lies can be complete without mentioning the insurance industry.

While discussing business, we are supposed to forget ethics, morality, conscience, duties and obligations to society, and the wide spectrum of truth and lies. We are in the realm of fantasy and dreams. As a popular song from the Hindi film *Jagate Raho* goes,

> *Life is but a dream,*
> *In the dream,*
> *What is lie, and my good man,*
> *What is truth?*

Insurance companies help us create our own estate, by selling life insurance as a lottery ticket, and help us protect our estate from catastrophic losses. In India, we had an army of demigods to do that, but in the US, we depend upon insurance companies. They are certainly quite good at protecting themselves. They don't assume any risk for an individual, but only distribute it among the rest of us. There is nothing wrong with that.

They invest the premiums we pay into stocks, certificates of deposit, commercial paper, and in real estate. Their sales force is mobile and their offices are in huge and ornate buildings. One of their magic tricks of profit is not to pay your claim or keep postponing it as much as they can.

An insurance policy is a *fine* instrument, in that it contains pages and pages of fine print that is mercifully kept microscopic. Even if you could, and rather would read it, you would not be able to understand what it means, especially to them; for, only that's what matters. I can tell you what the fine print says, regardless of the policy. It simply states that, *"This policy covers you against losses of all kind, except the one that you sustain."*

A good writer tries to convert his or her own experience into a universal one, to make it interesting to the reader. Here, I am describing my experience, unpleasant by definition, as an example of what you all have also gone through.

About a year and a half ago, several huge trees were toppled onto my family room by a wind storm, demolishing it entirely, and sparing me by a few seconds and a few inches. The insurance company made initial payments, withholding some money for depreciation. The first check had to be sent to the bank holding the mortgage on my house. It released some money to clear the debris, which was done.

We submitted modifications to their estimate and added a few more items for code compliance, architect's and filing fees, and for surveys, etc. Despite scores of my unanswered e-mails and phone calls and a complaint to the NYS Insurance Commission (a body as toothless as I would have been without the implants), after 18 months, still there is no trace of any civilization in my backyard.

I do not know how much I should budget for. The bank would not let me use the money to pay out the mortgage in part, and forget about restoring the family room. It wants me to pay it off completely. I cannot refinance the mortgage with them at a rate lower by 2%, nor can I rejuvenate the home equity line of credit until the reconstruction is completed.

Now, the insurance company holds $50-75,000 due me plus the depreciation, and the mortgagee bank holds an additional $40,000. My only option is to withdraw from my rapidly vanishing 403B plan, get the reconstruction done, and hope to get reimbursed someday, maybe. Meanwhile, the insurance company and the bank are enjoying my money. In fairness, I should say that the bank staff is sincerely doing its best to hand over the money to me.

Insurance companies can be more creative than con men. They try to sell us protection against everything and everybody except themselves and their agents. They push whole life insurance policies rather than term insurance, the so-called buyer's vis a vis renter's insurance. The whole life policy is more expensive for the client, but it generates much larger commissions for the sales agents.

The bait for that expensive policy is its savings element and its cash value with a provision for taking out a loan. A large percentage of these policies are closed or *surrendered* within first five years at a great loss to the buyer, who is by then five years older, and that much less insurable. Lure of savings and cash value ends up depriving the client of the protection that is much needed, and in an uncomplicated scenario, much cheaper to buy.

My own health insurance plan carrier just raised my co-pay for each prescription drug to $50 for a three months worth of supply, or $200 a year. We need to take maybe ten or more medications—see the *books information* on the last page to know why—for a possible co-pay of $2000 every year. No day-to-day drug should cost you more than $10 a month. Co-pay of several times that much is a sign of a much deeper disease lurking underneath, not in the patient, but in the healthcare insurance market.

17. THE SELF-CENTERED UNIVERSE

While talking about the role of the business, banks, insurance companies, or the stock market, we should not forget that all these are operated by people like you and me, merrily engaged in chasing our dream for a better tomorrow for ourselves and our children. These institutions are as greedy and evil as we all are, not an iota less, not more.

As Mahatma Gandhi said, "While pointing a finger towards someone else, remember that you are pointing three towards yourself." He also said in his saintly wisdom, "Do not be angry. If you are right, you do not need to, and if you are wrong, you cannot afford to." No matter how these institutions are, they are made in our images, and improving them has to begin with improving ourselves.

Our interests define which side we take in an argument. Our thinking changes with our changing perspective. What we like as a consumer, we may hate as a customer service person. We all like to keep our jobs, but we nonchalantly layoff our underlings to advance ourselves. We want governments to cut down spending, but not to eliminate our positions as teachers, sanitation workers, firefighters, or police officers.

When federal and state governments decrease their support for the local municipalities, the latter fire the police force, teachers, and firefighters first, before reducing the office staff. Traffic summonses increase, more red light surveillance cameras sprout up, and speed traps mushroom. It is the survival.

Businesses reducing their work force as a part of their cost cutting during the slower times, scarcely realize that essentially, they are making their customers and consumers unemployed, and hence forever unable to help the businesses raise their sales and ward off lean times.

It is hypocritical to advise government to refrain from creating jobs for the unemployed and to terminate their unemployment benefits, while expecting the same government to stand by with gold in its hands to help out the business, banks, and insurance companies, if and when they need it.

We, the consumers, have to choose between ecology and economy, and balance our needs realistically. We have to stay away from the all-too-prevalent NIMBY, or *not in my backyard* syndrome. We have to pull our own weight. We have to be free from that super selfish mentality.

Just about one hundred years ago, Mahatma Gandhi, then a practically unknown lawyer, wrote a very small book entitled, *Hind-Swaraj* (*Hind* as in *Mint*) or the Indian Self-Rule, in which he presented the blue print for the then colonial India to achieve its freedom by nonviolent means.

The book is in public domain now, and can be downloaded without charge from the internet. In that, Mr. Gandhi discusses the interplay of men and machines, and judicial use of the latter without jeopardizing the labor market.

Machines should take over monotonous and dangerous tasks, without idling the entire work force. Any profit made by making people lose their jobs is tainted with blood.

He has few kind words to say about the (British) parliament which he compares with a prostitute—to a great chagrin and anger of the British—carrying out the whims of any Prime Minister occupying the chair. We have our Congree, consisting of the house, and the Senate, which have no dearth of politicians who can be pocketed by the lobbyists.

It is easy for someone reading Mr. Gandhi's ideas hurriedly to conclude those to be outdated, impractical, idealistic, and irrelevant to our plight. The colonial India also understandably thought so. Although I disagree with those thinkers, I would not recommend following Mr. Gandhi's ideas without digesting them thoroughly. I can only suggest to study and think them through with an open mind.

Mr. Gandhi's greatest emphasis is on liberating his people from the mental slavery, something that we ought to emulate and learn to find our own solutions, pending any action from the government or the business. Keeping us preoccupied with that search may be at least as productive as occupying Wall Street.

18. CAPITALIST
CRIMES AGAINST AMERICA

It is essential to visualize Capitalism for what it is, that is, a colonial exploitative economic system that has turned upon its worshippers, treating them like its subjugated populace towards which it possibly cannot have any responsibility, duty, or obligation.

This unrecognized new face of Capitalism has enabled it to continue exploiting us by creating unemployment at home, exporting jobs abroad, making us "import" the products of our own companies and thereby increasing our national trade deficit.

Our businesses, banks, and insurance companies have made us pay dearly for our errors of judgment, and made us suffer generously for theirs as well.

Our system is working only for a fortunate few, enslaving the rest of us, the so-called *99 percent*. A very insignificant minority has usurped our freedom, our democracy, and its institutions.

This financial fascism has made the federal government with its executive and legislative branches unable to function effectively. It has corrupted our legislature enough to guarantee us a place of honor among the most corrupt nations. It is a miracle that the two *halves* (one percent against the 99 percent) of our financial house, divided against itself, are still standing.

It will be a much greater miracle if anything of any substance will come out of those commandeered institutions in time enough to be of some relevance. The upcoming major election in 2012 may bring more mud slinging to cloud our eyeglasses still more.

It is fashionable to propose conspiracy theories for our problems to sensationalize them. I will present one such theory here, if only to dismiss it right away for lack of evidence. It is quite plausible and theoretically attractive though.

The nation is entering the endgame of the 2012 Presidential elections. The fascist core comprising of big business and other vested interests is making a common cause against the President who has proved repeatedly that he can act decisively to make the change.

There is nothing illegal about contesting an election and winning people's minds and votes. It is quite something else, when a small group itself refuses to address the issues and stymies the government in doing so.

Insisting on tax cuts for the rich, cutting out all possible ways for government to fund its activities—abandoned by the other side anyway—and to progressively worsen the number, support system, and benefits for the unemployed, the latter made so by that group's own doing.

Moreover, in a *Mission Impossible* like master stroke, to blame the incumbent President for this failure, turn the shortsighted and selfish members of his own party and his voter base against its only hope—that is, to reelect him—would be very smart, only if it did not reek anti-American. Tell me it is not so, please!

There is no point in presenting here a wish list of what the business and the government can do, knowing very well that the latter cannot, and the former would not. We can only list what we may want them to do, and work on pressing those demands.

What the US Government Should do:

1. Ban the imports of goods manufactured by American companies in foreign lands. The Chinese and others can export their goods to us under the free trade policy. This will force American products to improve, and be competitive.

2. There must be an official way to remove these imports from the American companies from our *import* column, or to

levy penalizing import duties on these goods.

3. Withhold 25% of the money from their sales of such goods at home in lieu of any corporate income taxes due.

4. Alternatively, all payments should be made to their US offices and taxed appropriately. These last two items do not increase the corporate taxes, but they only improve their collection.

5. No amnesty should be offered to companies for bringing their money back to the US.

6. It should not insist that the companies it intends to bail out layoff thousands of their employees first.

7. Do not permit the bailed out businesses just look profitable by cutting their payroll liabilities. Improvement has to be real.

8. Assert the authority over the private sector that if the latter does not want to create jobs, the government would, because someone has to. There can be no leadership vacuum.

9. Reforms in the election system, its financing, and curtailing the influence of the lobbyists has to be demanded by people, as should be the measures against the corruption among the legislators.

10. If there are enough senators committed to never raising taxes, the government should exempt from paying any income tax, all those whose income falls below the cutoff for the Social Security, $110,001 for 2012.
11. Remove the *cap* on Social Security taxable earnings. That now becomes the level at which one reaches the maximum benefit, rather than the maximum contribution. Above that, the benefit does not increase.
12 Make the Social Security contributions tax deductible for all. Thus, the not so rich would also get some tax break. They rich will pay more but will get a larger deduction.

Thus, a person earning 80,000 a year pays no income tax, but pays nondeductible Social Security tax, and eventually collects benefit in line with contributions made.

One making $125,000 pays income tax but gets to deduct what (s)he paid to the Social Security, which will be more than what the first person paid, since there is no cap now. There will be more money in the Social Security fund, and the IRS can be reimbursed for the new tax deductions created, from the increased collection.

Capitalism, the Colonization of America

Someone making $500,000 will pay income tax, plus Social Security on the entire income, writing off the payment to the Social Security. In as much as we do not want to increase the government spending, the benefits should be same ($2,000 per person now) for everybody. The rich will pay more, will deduct more, and will get the same benefit.

What Business Should Do:

1. It is futile to expect business to be moral, ethical, and compassionate. However, it can learn to be really selfish in the long run. At present, it is shooting itself in the feet by increasing the unemployment.

2. Its mindset has to be retuned to appreciating that there is no difference between employees and consumers. One laid off employee removes ten shoppers from the mall. Conversely, by rehiring one employee, the business generates ten consumers. There is no other action that is more profitable and indicative of business acumen.

3. Businesses should not let its staff go just to raise the profits artificially, unless the business is running in the red.

4. Businesses that are not in near bankrupt condition may do well to rehire at least 10%

of their laid off workers. This is cheaper than any other way to create new markets, restore the faith in the markets, and stimulate the consumer spending.

5. Extending the unemployment benefits also returns a few more consumers to the shopping centers.

19. HEAL THYSELF!

In absence of any obvious healer, we ourselves have to treat our affliction. That do-it-yourself personal solution may not be adequate for the entire country, or even for oneself. It can only be the first step out of we do not know how many. My preference is for a nonviolent approach, especially since the enemy is within us, it is us.

We ourselves cannot create jobs easily, since we are the job seekers. We can certainly support the companies that are creating or at least preserving the jobs even during the downturn. Recently the New York Times ran a feature story on the Marvin Windows Products, manufacturer of energy efficient house windows.

Mr. Marvin's fourth generation descendants are now conducting their family business, the employees of which outnumber the population of the town housing it. During the last four years it has been losing money, but not their hearts. Not a single employee has been laid off, although a few have left because the overtime has disappeared.

Its CEO says that you cannot fire your way to prosperity. She also hits the proverbial nail right on its head when she says, "I don't have to worry about the Wall Street. We can absorb the losses, at least for a little longer."

What we *can* do:

1. Buying products made in America is the obvious thing to do, even if these products may be more expensive. Their improved sales may bring down their prices, we can hope.

2. Support the growing new lines of businesses like alternate forms of energy, biodegradable products, reusable and recyclable products.

When I was growing up in India, and during my early days in America, I used to hear that an American dog eats more meat than an average Indian. Ignoring that some Indians are vegetarian, that sure appeared to be a shame, although I still do not know quite whose.

The dog was certainly not to be blamed. When we hear about people in India, China, and elsewhere taking away our jobs, certainly it is not that they are coming here during the night, stealing the jobs, then leaving before the daybreak.

The truth is, our own companies are neatly packaging our jobs, taking them abroad, and selling there at a profit for themselves, exploiting the Indians and Chinese as well. Our companies never discriminate.

What causes unemployment here, causes inflation abroad by offering relatively higher wages by the local standards, and generate anti American feeling by giving lower wages compared to American standards. Like happiness, unhappiness also increases when shared indiscriminately.

3.   Styrofoam packaging material can be reused several times. I have reused the cardboard boxes from amazon.com after turning them inside out and resealing them to mail out my books. Turning them inside out removes all old barcodes and other insignia.

4.   Philosophical as this may sound, it is a sound philosophy. We do have to satisfy our needs, but our wants are a different story. The latter make us borrow money at 25-30% on our credit cards to enslave us.

5.   Our cable TV, pay per view programs, and downloads of various kind load us down. The cute little iPhone takes more money every month than the gas tank of our car.

6.   It makes no sense to finance anything that is going to lose its value, that is, *depreciate*.

The latest model car is going to lose 25% of its value the moment you take it out of the showroom. Buying a good used car, like the one coming off the lease, may be a better bet.

The idea behind all this is not only to save money by being thrifty. The point is that of not falling slaves to huge credit card debt and to the banks issuing that card. One may have to borrow money to attend a college, or maybe to buy a house which used to increase in value, but remember well, any debt enslaves you. Nowadays, almost all slavery is voluntary.

It would be quite unfortunate and simplistic for me to leave you with the US divided into two halves, one consisting of the filthy rich 1 percent of the population, mostly conservatives and Republicans. The other 99 percent being poor with more Democrats, and liberals.

We all belong to one or the other side depending upon the time of the day, and the constellation ruling our birth sign. All my poor compatriots were Democrats when they became citizens of the US, to turn Re-publication abruptly on amassing their first one hundred thousand dollars. The latter can make us do anything. We can say quite accurately, "The D-bill made me do it!"

Businesses, banks, and brokerages are our institutions and there is nothing wrong in patronizing them, provided they show some social sense of responsibility.

7.   If a company has been penalized for misinforming or outright defrauding its customers and clients and is reporting filthy profits, I would not want to support it by patronizing it or by owning its appreciating stock soaked with blood.

8.   There is no reason why we cannot demand that stock exchanges to delist these companies and refuse to trade their stock say, three months after their conviction for such crimes. Three months are given to let the shareholders dump their holdings at plummeting prices. It should never be rewarding to be partners in crime by holding its shares.

9.   Companies sitting on idle cash instead of hiring will not deserve my business. Those lobbying for wrong causes like tobacco subsidies deserve the same approach.

10.   Similarly, businesses laying off their staff, keeping stock prices high, and rewarding their CEOs will see me sell their stocks.

11. Avoid paying fees to banks for minimum balances, bill payment, using their ATMs, or getting a certified check, etc. Go to a credit union instead.

12. If businesses are not willing to stop laying off and resume rehiring their employees, we should move the government to use its muscles. It should not be forgotten that the government is paying the unemployment benefits, and is not receiving any payroll taxes from unemployed people. The latter are not flocking to malls and paying the sales tax either. Only putting them to work can correct these.

13. Government should not force layoffs. When the federal government bailed out General Motors, the latter was forced to lay off thousands of employees as a pre-requisite. Not bad for a government that is trying desperately to persuade corporations not to lay off their employees!

14. Any institution requiring bailout at tax payers' expense should restore its staffing level before being allowed to reward its CEOs.

15. Any business laying off employees should lower the pay of its CEO by 50%. There is nothing to gain by preventing food stamp money being wasted on Coca-Cola, if we

are going to give billions to the intoxicated banks.

To achieve any of the above, we have to have the central government that can act freely, without interference from bought out politicians and strong lobbies of myriad kinds. That is too much to hope for. Beneficiaries of abuses are not going to act to curtail them.

16. *This item is dedicated to the memories of my dad, who was a lower middle class merchant of lose tea in Mumbai (Bombay then), and had one free-lance laborer and another employee, a 75 year old senior man.*

When the business ran into trouble, thanks to natural and political turmoil, my dad got ill and felt compelled to close it. He did not even have to give one month's notice. However, he called the senior man, explained the situation to him, which the latter also knew well, and asked him to look for another job.

He did not lay him off, but continued to run the losing business. The employee asked my dad to go ahead and close the business, without worrying about him. My dad told him that it would not be easy for the latter to find a job at his advanced age. Maybe, after six months or so, he landed a job, when my dad closed the shop, and went looking for a job for himself! He could afford to be rich, because he had no money.

17. Stop giving money directly or indirectly to any organization that supports causes (depending upon your preference) like tobacco, guns, environmental scofflaws, political religious groups, foreign lobbies, etc.

18. Seek legislation to prevent exploiting Medicare and Medicaid benefits and other public programs.

19. Be careful about whom you vote into sensitive offices. Do not export corrupt local politicians to Washington, D.C. Do not support any candidate for a national office that pledges his or her commitment to any special interest group putting its own agenda above the national interest.

20. Get involved with public watchdog groups, and public interest lobbies.

21. Do not spoil anybody by giving free services. Volunteer judiciously. Charity is supposed to be given to the needy and worthy only.

Do not fall for semantic cynicism and playing with canned words like this ism or that, or rightist or leftist, pro this or anti that, liberal or conservative, etc., and divide the divided house still more.

Once in power, all parties will spend our money, and will cater to the special groups that brought them to power. All will tax us progressively more disguising it cleverly.

John Hancock and others officially started the struggle for our independence in 1776. Thomas Jefferson then tried unsuccessfully to do away with slavery, but that had to wait for arrival of President Lincoln *four scores and seven years* later.

Jefferson pledged an *eternal hostility against all kinds of tyranny over the minds of men*, and declared, *These thirteen colonies are, and of necessity ought to be free and independent nations.*

Let us replace *thirteen* with *fifty*, for inflation, and rid ourselves of subjugation of the colonial era Capitalist system and usher in the reformed Capitalist or another system better suited for a free country. The revolution to restore the glory and the spirit of America continues with constant vigilance. That is the price for liberty!

BOOKS BY BHARAT S. SHAH, M.D.

Sanskrit: An Appreciation without Apprehension
(Includes *A Crash Course to Learn the Devanagari Script*
Second edition. Our bestseller on the internet) $24

An Introduction to Jainism
(Second edition. Our bestseller on the internet) $18
(First edition, while the supplies last) $15

Programmed Text to Learn Gujarati (Second edition) $20

A Crash Course to Learn the Gujarati Script $3

A Crash Course to Learn the Devanagari Script
(Used for Sanskrit, Hindi, and Marathi languages) $3

English for the Grandma (In Gujarati) $15

Sameepe (A documentary popular novel,
the original version of "Dawn at Midnight," in Gujarati.
Not available on Internet. Please Email the author) $10

PUBLICATIONS DURING 2011-2012

Dawn at Midnight (A documentary novel on awaiting
liver transplant) $12
Dawn at Midnight (*Kindle E-book*) $7

My Life with Panic Disorder (A documentary novel) $10
My Life with Panic Disorder (Kindle E-book) $6

Questions Answers Exclamations:
From the Garage of a Clinical Researcher
Author's ideas for medical research being bequeathed
to the future generation. $15

Capitalism, colonization of America,
and Mating Habits of the Praying Mantis (Paper)   *$8*
(*Kindle E-book*) $5

All these books are in English, unless noted otherwise. They
are available from retailers like amazon.com. Their detailed
descriptions, cover images, sample pages, readers' reviews,

Setubandh Publications
1 Lawson Lane, Great Neck, NY 11023-1042
1 (516) 482-6938
Email: <bhrtshah@yahoo.com>

comments, and shipping information, are available on website of amazon.

www.ingramcontent.com/pod-product-compliance
Lightning Source LLC
Chambersburg PA
CBHW051337170526
45166CB00002B/858